Ghost Stor City

By

Kitty Mervine

Illustrated by Noah Whippie

Dedicated to all of the citizens of Keene, both living and not quite dead

First Edition

Copyright 2017

Introduction

The first problem when writing a book about 'ghosts', is that there is no real agreement on the definition of 'ghost'. Ghosts might be the spirits of the dead, trapped here on Earth or ghosts could also be a memory or imprint of an occurrence that took place at one time while a person was alive. A bump in the night to some Keene residents means the cat has knocked something over, but to others it means the house ghost is out and about. Reported ghosts were found to be evil or happy, friendly or sad, or just a loud hot water heater. If nothing else, what living humans define as 'ghost' covers quite a broad spectrum.

The people of Keene aren't interested, in most cases, in getting rid of their ghosts. Sharing your house with a spirit in Keene is not uncommon at all. One family reported 'She was here long before we were, we just tolerate her moods. She's a part of the family and we would miss her if she were gone.'

The stories reported here are of course unproven. These stories should be considered folklore, not proof of life after death. Names have been changed and some locals are not given. The reason is that while a family may be fine with sharing a ghost story today, tomorrow they may wish to sell their home. While Keene is tolerant of ghosts, home buyers tend to shy away from ghosts. We did not wish to inflict any monetary or mental anguish on anyone kind enough to share their stories.

The book is far from comprehensive; there are ghosts that are jealously guarded by those that are busy 'investigating' them. Many stories were family secrets, but not ours to share. We hope these stories will give the ghost enthusiast a hint of just some of the rich ghost lore of Keene.

Keene's Own Alice

Robin Hood Park and Keene's Own Alice

Keene's Robin Hood Park is an oasis for children of all ages. In the summer, there is a playground and a chance to hike trails gentle enough for even a preschooler to manage. Winter brings ice skating and, over the years, many Keene children have learned to skate on the water reservoir located there.

The park was founded by one of the more altruistic of Keene's citizens, George Wheelock, as a place for children to enjoy nature. The original twelve acres he donated were named 'The Children's Woods', and a later donated eighty-three acres were called 'Robin Hood Park'.

However, even this most child-friendly of parks has a reported spirit or two living there. The spirit of this story is a child. Several mothers speak of seeing a small girl along the paths, dressed as if she were going to a fancy party. The little spirit-girl seems stuck in time, with her flat leather shoes and apron that protects her light-colored dress from stains. It is her attire that has earned her the name Alice after the title character in *Alice in Wonderland*. Alice peeks out from behind the trees and the many large boulders in the park. While children are delighted with glimpses of Alice, parents aren't always so comfortable.

One mother, Elaine, told me the story of her daughter Molly. Molly was a typical tomboy, until one day she wandered off to explore the pathways of Robin Hood Park. Elaine explained, 'I would sit on a rock, bring a book and just keep an ear out for her. We would go fairly early in the morning when the park was very quiet. I could always hear Molly chatting away saying 'hello' to squirrels and talking to herself.'

Elaine noticed a change one day when Molly came down wearing one of her Disney Princess outfits. 'Her grandmother would send them to her, and Molly had little interest in them. I would dress her up in the costume and take a photograph to send my mom. Molly was a dynamo then, my little tornado, and wearing a dress would just have slowed her down.'

Elaine questioned why Molly would want to wear a princess dress to the park, and Molly explained her new friend Alice wanted her to wear a pretty dress so they could 'look like sisters.' There were usually no other children at the park so early. 'I would often go then, just so Molly could wear herself out, and when we went back later on in the afternoon she was much calmer playing with the other children.' Elaine, being an easy-going mother, allowed Molly to wear her princess dress, but insisted on her wearing sneakers.

From then on, Molly insisted on wearing dresses for her early morning park explorations and would speak of her friend, Alice. Elaine assumed that Molly had a wonderful imaginary friend; Molly had seen an *Alice in Wonderland* movie and she had been looking for a rabbit hole at Robin Hood Park. Elaine grew more nervous when she began to pay more attention to what Molly was saying at the park.

'Molly had long conversations with Alice,' she shared. 'They would talk about school, pets. It was all one-sided, but Molly would do long pauses and seemed to be replying to direct questions from Alice.' Elaine worried this was perhaps too much fantasy, so she put down her book and tagged along.

Elaine was intrigued when she walked with Molly, and Molly pointed to a rock and said the name of the rock was Jumbo. Elaine laughingly replied it was indeed a jumbo-sized boulder, but Molly said, 'No, the rock is named Jumbo, Alice told me.' Elaine looked more closely and noticed some carving on the rock. 'I took out my car keys, and scraped away at the letters which were covered with some sort of green moss.' Elaine was shocked to find the name, JUMBO, clearly carved into the boulder. Molly named other boulders, and each time Elaine looked, she saw the faint etchings of the name carved into the rock. 'I never even knew the rocks had names, or that someone had the names inscribed on the rocks.'

When Elaine asked how she knew the names, Molly would insist, 'Alice did...she knows all the rocks.' Elaine lost her temper with Molly, certain that some adult had told Molly the names and stories of the boulders of Robin Hood Park. Elaine spoke to a few of the other parents at the park; none had spoken to Molly, and some of them claimed to get a creepy feeling when walking the paths.

Elaine didn't stop taking Molly, because the park is wonderful. 'I enjoyed finding out some of the rocks have names, but I kept a close eye on Molly, and saved my reading for when she took her afternoon nap.' Elaine continued to take Molly to where Alice spoke to her. She felt if Alice were the ghost of a little girl then, 'Alice might be sad with no one to visit her. I thought if anything happened to Molly, and she were stuck here as a ghost, I would want her to have friends.'

Molly spoke to Alice for the rest of that summer, and would ask her mother why she couldn't see Alice. Elaine told Molly to ask Alice. Alice told Molly that she could only appear to children, and that one day even Molly wouldn't be able to play with her anymore.

The next summer, Molly went to the park in her shorts, t-shirt, and sneakers, and didn't mention Alice at all. Elaine asked Molly about Alice and she responded, 'Oh, I must have grown up too much!'

If Alice is truly a playful, well-dressed, spirit at Robin Hood Park, I hope she finds many future generations of children to play with until they have 'grow up too much.'

Woodlawn Cemetery: Keep it Clean

The most haunted location in Keene is reputed to be near the Knight Summer Chapel, which is part of Woodlawn Cemetery. The area is a favorite for those with cameras trying to capture photographs of orbs and other ghostly subjects. It is reported that the spirit of a little girl will peek at you from behind tombstones and trees.

Traditional folklore says you must never curse near the chapel, or you will taste soap in your mouth. This soapy discipline comes from a ghost that objects to cursing, and will try to clean your mouth. This rumored ghostly punishment means that people are often around the chapel, cursing away hoping for a ghostly, and possibly soapy, encounter.

So many stories abound, that it's hard to choose just one to feature.

This story can perhaps be representative of all the strange events near the chapel. A group of bored teenagers went to the Knights Chapel to see if a ghost would wash their mouths out with soap. Keene is a lovely town, but a bit dull for young people, though I'm surprised this was their best option for entertainment. Still, what could be more fun than to test this ghostly myth? So the five young people piled into a car, drove to the cemetery, and parked near the chapel.

The five were all teenagers and two of them were a new couple. At first, everyone just cursed away, with three claiming, 'I can taste the soap; it is really awful!' The taste did not stop the teens from cursing. As could be expected, it made them curse even more. The only two who did not taste soap were the young couple. They were teased by the others, that they were 'too sweet' for the ghost. The couple retorted that they were too smart to fall for this trick. They were sure the others were just imagining the soapy taste. Finally, the couple was challenged to curse as much and as creatively as they possibly could. The couple faced the chapel and yelled out curses and insults for almost a full minute, and at the end, they just laughed and claimed to taste nothing. Their friends suggested the couple French kiss, so they could taste if there was soap in each other's mouths.

What happened next, at first seemed very innocent. The couple kissed deeply, embracing each other tightly. The couple kept kissing and kissing, until their friends began to joke 'get a room!' The deep kiss continued.

The couple then tried to push away from each other and soon they were using all their strength to break off the kiss, even digging their feet into the ground. Their deep kiss was endless, their lips locked, as if a powerful magnet held them together. At first, the three friends thought the couple was joking, but soon were convinced otherwise, by the terror in their eyes.

They ran over and began to pull the couple apart. It was only when one of the teens shouted, 'They are sorry! We're sorry! We won't do this again, let them go!' that the couple broke apart.

The couple fell to the ground, exhausted, and catching their breaths in deep gulps. They later said they did not taste soap, but ashes. 'It was like eating smoke from a campfire or from hell.' They could not break apart, and were having trouble breathing. The young woman felt as if a bony hand were holding her head in place. The young man refused to talk about the experience ever again. The group left the cemetery, and warned their friends not to bother the chapel ghosts.

So, go visit Woodlawn Cemetery, but please be respectful. If you aren't, the residents there will be sure to let you know they like to be left in peace.

Heartless

The Zombie Without a Heart

Fortune tellers and psychics comment that they have a tough time in Keene. A few have reported they have better readings outside of Keene, and that they sometimes have nightmares after attending a psychic fair in town. Things go wrong: batteries run out of power, lights flicker, things they were sure they packed, go missing. And they dream. Some dreams are of two young men, who are angry at those who cast fortunes. Others are dreams of a zombie: a young man who is looking for his eternal rest. Perhaps the men have good reason to be angry, if those young men are Isaac and Samuel, who lived in Keene in the early 1800's.

Seth and Adam's brother, Isaac, was dying. They had recently lost another brother, Samuel, to the same disease. Consumption, or what we would now call Tuberculosis (TB), was a leading killer before the introduction of antibiotic treatment in the 1940's.

The endless coughing that would bring up blood was a sure sign that death was near. Since the cause was unknown, attempts to cure the disease varied widely and were almost always ineffective. Seth and Adam, having lost one brother already, were willing to try anything. Desperate for a cure, they went to a fortune teller in Keene and asked for advice.

When traditional medicine fails, even today, people will seek the help of alternative medicine. This, however, was the early 1800's and your local doctor could often do as much harm as good. The fortune teller the young men turned to was more than willing to take their money for her bad advice. When the local doctor said there was nothing to do, the seer gave the boys something to do. Hope was bought at a high price for this working-class family.

The fortune teller gave the young men a cure that was gruesome, but she swore it would work. Seth and Adam were to dig up the body of their recently deceased brother, Samuel. They were then to take out his heart, and feed it to their ill brother, Isaac. Samuel, the seer claimed, was not at rest. His spirit was still alive. If the family could feed that spirit to Isaac, via the heart, he would regain his strength.

The fortune teller claimed that Samuel had cursed the family for not curing him, and that only by destroying his heart would his spirit rest and not claim the life of Isaac. If this was not done, each brother would die off, one by one, and the spirit of Samuel would haunt Keene forever.

The brothers followed her directions: dig up their brother from his grave in the middle of the night, careful to hide it from watching eyes. They were shocked to find Samuel's body looking as if they had just buried him. Some versions of the story have Samuel looking even better than when he had been buried an emaciated corpse. Samuel looked like the fit and strong, young man he was before his illness.

Seth and Adam worked quickly, cutting into the body and retrieving the heart. The heart itself was not withered and dried, but plump and wet. The brothers then reburied the body, and went home to make a meal of the heart for their sick brother and, when they cut into the heart, fresh liquid spurt out.

Sadly, the cure did not work, and Isaac soon died. Seth and Adam were angry. The fortune teller had not only taken their money, but she had caused them to desecrate the grave of Samuel. They went to demand their money back from the crooked seer, but could find no sign of her. The small hut where the fortune teller lived was empty and it looked as if it had been ransacked. Furniture and plates had been smashed and broken into small bits. The brothers were accused of having attacked the fortune teller, as she was never seen again. But they always claimed someone else with a grievance had cheated them of their revenge.

The brothers prepared Isaac for his burial, much as they had done for Samuel not long before. The night Isaac died, a frost had come and the ground had frozen. As is tradition, even today in parts of New Hampshire, Isaac's body was put in a grave vault to await a thaw when the ground could be opened to receive his body.

It was then that that the problems started for Keene. Young men walking late at night would feel a sudden chill, and turn to find a young man following them. The young man appeared to be normal, except for a hole in the middle of his body. This was before streetlights, so the descriptions are based on what could be seen from a carried lantern or just the moonlight. Also, since many of these young men were returning from taverns, the stories were treated as a joke.

There was one young man, tipsy enough, to challenge the man with the hole in his chest. The brave, but drunk man claimed he was then attacked by a demon that tried to tear out his heart. The sightings stopped soon after this, and people wondered if the stories were just imagined or had something otherworldly happened?

The spring thaw came and Seth and Adam were preparing to oversee the internment of their brother Isaac. When the body was brought out from the grave vault, to everyone's surprise, Isaac's body had been mutilated. A gaping hole was where his heart should have been. The brothers quickly buried Isaac, and the story remained buried in family legend until now.

Did Keene have a zombie, looking to replace his own stolen heart? Also, why was the body of Samuel so fresh? Could it be the cold chill of fall weather preserving his body, or was Samuel something else from New England legend?

Fortune tellers of the time were known to recommend such remedies for curing illnesses. There are many written accounts of this happening all over New England, but this family story of what happened is especially chilling. Let's hope Samuel and Isaac continue to rest in peace, even if fortune tellers and psychics of today may still be haunted by the brothers.

Harriet Huntress Just Wants Respect

Keene has many ghost stories, but one of the most popular seems to be that of Harriet Huntress; the namesake and resident ghost of Huntress Hall on the campus of Keene State College. An abandoned wheelchair in the attic of the Hall is a part of the inspiration for the ghostly legend. Of course, no one is sure just who the owner of the wheelchair was, or why it's sitting in the attic, but it makes for a great story.

One common theory, as told by several former students, is that Harriet Huntress does not like to be made fun of. Students who dress up like her for Halloween, usually in a gray wig and some sort of wheeled chair, find Harriet is not amused, and she will have her revenge. Things happen to those who make fun of Keene's best-known ghost.

There is almost always some form of retribution, especially to those who would imitate her ghostly presence. She's fond of tripping any student who makes fun of the wheelchair. Huntress saves her more extreme revenge for those who would wheel a cart down a hallway trying to scare others. One student and his friends, attempted to scare fellow students, by making haunting noises. He did not believe in ghosts or curses before he took part in the hoax, but all who participate had troubles within the week of the event. He broke his leg, another student had a bad car accident, and another had a car that wouldn't start and needed expensive repairs. A fourth slipped on an ice-covered sidewalk and threw out his back so badly he needed to use a wheelchair for the rest of the semester.

The student felt that Harriet saved this especially appropriate revenge for that young man, as he was the mastermind of the hoax.

Does Harriet Huntress still roam the hall that bears her name in a wheelchair?   Perhaps...or perhaps she just doesn't like people making fun of her. No matter what, it's better to just be polite, and not make fun of people...even if they are dead!

Every Parent's Nightmare

The Blood-Stained Floor

The rich history of Keene, the town itself dating back to 1735, is the stuff of pride for the residents. This pride is shown by the care residents take in preserving the old homes that have seen the cycle of life played through, over the generations. Perhaps hidden in a home is an unspoken story that is part of the history of almost any town.

The house of this story is circa 1920's. It is currently empty, though there are plans for it to be rented out soon. I met the owner, a man in his early 40's, at the front door. Mark assured me the home was safe, but wanted me to see the bloody floor.   I was fine with just hearing his story as my goal is to document ghost stories as folklore, not prove or disprove them. Mark insisted that I see the floor. It seemed important to him that I believe the story of what his family went through.

Mark bought the home as a 'flip' about four years ago. 'I was going to do most of the work myself. I grew up doing this kind of work. I figured, a year, at most two, I'd make an easy profit.' Things didn't quite go as planned. 'My wife (Gloria) got pregnant, and then she couldn't work. I had to take as much overtime as I could at my job to make up the income. We gave up our apartment and just moved into the home while I worked on it. It was slow going; I worked on the bathrooms and kitchen first so we could use the place. The bedrooms were just ugly, so they were going to be last.'

As soon as they moved into the house, Gloria started having nightmares. She would wake up at night to the sounds of women crying and Mark figured it was just being pregnant. Mark decided that with the baby coming, he might cheer his wife up if he skipped some of the downstairs and worked on the baby's room.

Mark explained that when you work on a room, you work from the top to bottom. The last thing done is to remove old carpet or refinish a floor. The nursery was stripped of ugly wallpaper and repainted when Mark decided to tear up the old carpeting. 'It's like the lottery,' he explained. 'You don't know what's going to be under there, but you hope it's good, wood flooring you can refinish.'

Under the carpet was good, wood flooring, but there were also several brown and black stains. 'There were some spots where it looked like it had been a lot of something, I dunno, like it had dripped all over. It wasn't like those crime scene splatters; this was a lot of dripping. One area near the center of the room had the worst of the stains. There was this old coconut matting under the carpet, that had a lot of stains, but the stains in the one area of the wood flooring were really deep. I refinished the floor anyway, but I bought a rug to cover the stains in the center of the room.'

Gloria kept having dreams about women crying and she also began to see things. Out of the corner of her eye, she would see a middle-aged woman and also an older man. Mark described it as 'almost there' and 'she knew when they were around. They let her know.'

Mark's wife felt sorry for the crying women, but she wasn't afraid of them. However, the older man and middle-aged woman scared his wife. Mark hoped once the baby came, his wife would calm down. He didn't worry until he started to clean out the crawl space attic. 'I found stuff up there I didn't like.' Mark showed me what he had found and later brought downstairs. It was doctor's equipment from the 1920's. There was a green, metal, folding table, some old clamps and surgical instruments. There were also lights with large, metal, bowl-like shades.

Mark figured the room had been some sort of doctor's office, though he thought it was odd to have a surgery in a bedroom, rather than on the first floor. Mark spoke of his findings with a neighbor who then told a story that he'd heard of the house.

It was rumored that abortions had been performed at the home by the couple who lived there. Mark felt a chill go through him when he heard this. Mark and Gloria aren't against abortion. 'I know that my wife's pregnancy was a real surprise for us. We wondered how we could afford just one baby. I can't blame someone, long ago. How did you keep having kids? There wasn't much choice back then. I wondered, though, about someone who would perform abortions. My wife, it wasn't the women that upset her, it was that couple. I decided not to tell her the rumor.'

Mark felt the last thing Gloria needed was to add to her anxiety and stress. 'We had to live here,' he points out, 'I didn't have the money to move us. I still didn't believe anything was going on.'

The baby came, and things became worse for his wife. She insisted the baby sleep in the room with them, and seemed afraid to leave the baby with a sitter. 'My mom, her sister…. family wasn't allowed to babysit. My wife had to be with the baby in the house. It was only when we took the baby outside the house that she relaxed. She talked to her doctor, and the doctor thought maybe she had some of that baby depression. He put her on some medicine and told us to put the baby in the nursery and get out more.'

When the baby was put in the nursery, Mark would find Gloria sleeping on the floor near the crib in the morning. 'She would swear she didn't remember how she got there. She would sleep walk.' Mark just thought it was the depression, until the one night he awoke to hear his wife calling out his name.

Mark found his wife standing in the nursery holding the baby, and Mark finally saw the couple for himself. 'There were these dark shadows, near the crib. The one shadow, it seemed to be reaching out toward my family. I just lost it.' Mark wasn't scared. Instead, he felt this huge, black, anger overtake him. 'I just yelled at them to leave my baby alone, and ran over and picked up the crib. I picked up this heavy crib and just threw it. Everything went all over the place. It was crazy….just crazy.' Mark still can't explain his anger. He finally believed his wife, and he had to protect his family.

He packed up his family and they went to stay with his parents. Only Mark has returned to the house. 'We're renting a new home; it's only about ten-years old. I'm done with old homes. I don't know what happened here, or what is happening, but I'm done with this place.' He is finishing the renovations as he can, getting the home ready to rent until the housing market picks up again. 'Then I'm selling this. I'll get what I can out of it. I have to make back something.'

I asked if he'd be selling to a young family, maybe a family with a baby. Mark shakes his head, 'I have to take care of my family, so I'm not going to promise anything. I hope maybe the next family is Catholic or something, or they can get some of those ghost people to figure this out. I'm not doing that, I'm just telling you as I want someone to hear this story. There is something bad here. It's not my problem now, but it's like a war story. Do I believe in ghosts? I don't know what is in this house. I just know my family isn't coming back.'

I looked at the nursery. The crib was still lying on the floor: half-broken, resting on its side, but the rest of the baby furniture, clothing and toys are gone. Mark rolled back the light-beige, area rug that covered most of the floor. Sure enough, there were dark stains. Mark showed me where he gouged into the wood, to see how deep the stains went. He suggested that maybe, 'some of that crime scene stuff that, maybe, could show if it's really blood. I don't care anymore.'

Mark and his wife and child are doing well now. Everyone finally sleeps through the night. Mark is going to install wall-to-wall carpeting in the old nursery.

The Mirror's Reflective Predictions

Not all of Keene's spooky stories involve ghosts; this is one such story.

Court Street in Keene is known for the beautiful, old houses. While many have been converted into apartments or offices, there are still a few privately-owned homes. The setting for this next story takes place at one of these houses that is now just a shadow of the home it was long ago. When you visit, you will notice a bit of gingerbread trim has fallen off, slate shingles have slid off parts of the roof, and the front stairs lean a bit to the side. Stepping onto the front porch, you will find that the boards creak loudly announcing your arrival before you have a chance to ring the old-fashioned, winding doorbell, located in the center of the large, oak door.

My visit was to find out more about a mysterious mirror that has been housed here for over 100 years.

I was welcomed by a home-health assistant, Mary. She had contacted me about her client who had a story to share. Mary wasn't sure she believed the story of the mirror, but said, 'I've never been brave enough to go see it for myself!' Mary warned me her client, Ava, was quite old and I was not to expect too much from her, but she thought Ava would get a kick out of sharing her story.

I was shown into a quiet bedroom on the second floor. There was a modern hospital bed, but the rest of the furniture seemed as old as the inhabitant of the room. It was all made of a dark, carved wood. There was no mirror above the dresser with the bow-front drawers, and the walls were void of paintings and prints. It was a plain room with sheer curtains over the windows. Despite the sunny day, the room was dark. The trees were in full foliage and gave the room a green, comforting glow, reminding me almost of being inside an aquarium.

Sitting in an old-fashioned, padded, rocking chair was the woman with the story. Ava waved a hand at a cane-bottomed chair nearby and invited me to sit down and I explained I wanted to document her story. She was happy to share as long as I promised that I wouldn't 'bring people around. They can believe me or not. I don't care. But I'll tell you as long as you promise to go see the mirror.' I had no clue what the story would turn out to be, but I was skeptical enough to take her challenge and I agreed to see the mirror.

First, though, Ava had to tell her story.

When she was younger, Ava and her siblings lived on the third floor. It was the nursery. There were five children, and they all slept together in two rooms. There was a third bedroom for the woman who helped to look after the children. 'We didn't have a nanny,' Ava pointed out. 'We had a woman who helped our mother run the house and chase after all of us.' Ava and her sister, Jane, were the only girls. The three boys slept in one room, and she and Jane shared another.

The third floor was still filled with all the old furniture from this home that has been owned by the same family for generations. The girls' bedroom still had the old-fashioned iron beds, two twin-sized ones, which Ava and Jane slept in. Ava said their room also had the mirror. No one was sure when or how the mirror came to be in the house. All Ava knew is that one day Jane found the almost full-sized mirror, when she was exploring the attic. Their brothers to helped Jane drag it down to her room and cleaned it up so she would have someplace to 'preen and look at how pretty she was.'

Jane soon found that the mirror had some weird characteristics. While Jane could see how beautiful she was, she also said that if you kept looking at the mirror, it would slowly change to reflect what you would look like in years to come. Jane found herself changing from young teenager to old woman, if she looked long enough.

A first, this frightened Jane. 'She told me everything. We were born ten months apart. We were often mistaken for twins. She liked to boss me around, but she also knew she could tell me any secret.'

The girls decided to ask their grandmother about the mirror. Ava said her grandmother was in her late 80's at the time, and knew all the family secrets. Their grandmother told them the mirror had been hidden away as it disturbed people. When pressed, her grandmother admitted some felt the mirror had the ability to show people how old they will be when they die.

After that, Jane didn't mind the mirror anymore. The reflection was that of a very old woman, and that was all that Jane needed to feel that she was invincible. She felt she could not die before she was very old. Jane began to take risks and became 'Wild!' The mirror gave her the courage to travel and to take chances, and Ava admired her freedom.

I asked Ava what she saw when she had looked in the mirror. Ava laughed, 'I forgot to tell you, when I was a child, I was almost completely blind. That's another reason I was so close to Jane. She was my eyes to the world.' Things changed when Ava had an operation in the 1970's that allowed her to regain part of her eyesight. Jane wanted Ava to look in the mirror. She was rather nervous to do so, but that Jane was bossy as always.

Ava had regained only partial sight, but it was good enough for her to see, clearly reflected, her own self. 'I was so happy to be able to see, that I wasn't tired of looking at myself yet,' she joked. Then, just as her sister claimed, Ava saw the image in the mirror slowly begin to change. Ava found herself looking at an old woman. Jane was standing beside her and suddenly became angry. Jane no longer saw herself reflected as an old woman, but as she was. Ava and Jane were middle-aged then, and Jane started screaming, 'Why am I not OLD! Why are you OLD!' Jane became so upset that she hit the mirror with her fist, cracking it slightly.

Ava and Jane were the only two family members still living in the home at that time. They hosted their brothers and their families during holidays, and kept the place up as best they could. While Jane was difficult, they had always been close. But after the mirror incident, Jane had only anger towards Ava. 'She thought somehow I had stolen her reflection from her, perhaps because we were almost like twins. Perhaps the mirror had been confused or mistaken. All I know is that Jane changed. She began to be more careful, and she became afraid to leave the house. Just when I was ready to do things in life because I could see, Jane gave up on life.'

Sadly, the mirror did not lie, as Jane did die in a car accident six months after the incident. Ava sighed, 'I blame myself, as I told her to stop moping around and go out. She went to visit our nephew, and died in a car accident while she was in Arizona visiting his family. She was in her early 60's, and I try not to feel too sorry for her. She lived a really exciting life because of that mirror. It doesn't matter how old you live, it matters how you live. She didn't need a mirror to teach her that!'

At this point I was rather nervous, but I was still willing to go up another flight of stairs to see the mirror. 'Mary is too scared to even look,' Ava chuckled. Sure enough, it was all as Ava said. The old iron bed and the mirror in a corner. The mirror was spotted with age, and the silver backing was coming off in places. There was even the small crack where Jane had hit the mirror. 'It's not a very good mirror anymore for reflecting reality,' she said. I went over with Ava to look, and saw only myself as I was. I wondered if that was a good or bad sign. The darkened room with the poorly-reflecting mirror began to play tricks on my eyes, though. I thought I saw myself, but with more wrinkles and slightly stooped over. The longer I looked, the less sure I was about what was being reflected. The spooky atmosphere and story, combined with my imagination to create a reflection that seemed to change every few moments. I found myself looking away with relief, unsure of just what I had seen. I still didn't know what to think, other than I had been quite scared for a few moments.

I asked Ava what she saw. She stood before the mirror. 'I see an old woman, just what I've been seeing all those years since my eye operation. She hasn't changed a bit!'

I took Ava back down to her room and thanked her for her hospitality. Ava assured me I probably hadn't looked at the mirror long enough to know my fate, but reminded me, 'It didn't do Jane any good in the end. You have to live like you have a long life waiting for you. You can't hide away from whatever might happen. The only thing we know is we don't know how long we'll be here.'

Or as in the case of Ava, she knows her time is up soon but I am glad she still had time left to share the story of the mysterious mirror.

Speed Demon

Arch Street Tunnel: Skull Speeder

Arch Street is known as a quiet drive to and from Keene. Going to Keene you pass a farm, and then pass under the old railroad arch tunnel. It's a bit tricky; you have to slow down, as there isn't room for two cars to be in the tunnel at the same time. Still, it's a popular shortcut to get to the high school or west side of town.

It is not popular with everyone, as many people avoid driving there. The reasons given seem to be all concerned with safety. Certainly, in winter the slope of the street past the farm is a reason for concern; It quickly becomes slick in a snow or ice storm and is best avoided then.

The concerns reported all center around the tunnel. There is something that makes folks uncomfortable about driving there, even in the daytime. Some claim that there have been many deaths there. It does appear to be an area you would want to be very careful, but certainly not someplace to avoid. I drive this road often, and have found that most people are very careful when approaching the tunnel, and slow down...or attempt to.

My own odd experience with this road happened when I was pulled over for speeding. My family jokes that I was born driving like a grandmother. My fear of speed was learned at a young age, when I was told what a speeding ticket would do to my insurance. I was informed by my family that if I got a speeding ticket, I would have to pay for all my car insurance. Since I knew I could not afford that, I began my life-long habit of driving slightly under the speed limit at all times. This annoys people, so I have learned to pull over every now and again to allow others to pass me. It's a habit I can't break. One day, though, I did break the habit while driving by the farm. I zipped through the tunnel without stopping to check for traffic. 'You didn't even slow down!' was the first comment from the officer who pulled me over. I blamed it on daydreaming. I was obviously not drunk and, though confused, apologized. The officer let me off with a verbal warning. He commented that folks like to speed up on this road. He did say 'You have to be careful...I don't know what it is, but people drive different here.'

As stories began to come in about the bridge and the road, I found the police officer was correct; people do drive differently on this road. There are over fifty accounts concerning speeding, drivers' faces changing, and ghostly apparitions that have occurred when driving near the tunnel.

The stories almost all include a reference of feeling 'uncomfortable' or 'finding myself speeding.' One story that stood out, took place in the 1950's.

Helen was a teenager and she jokes that she never liked Mike until he got a car. Mike lived next door to her in Keene, and she never had time for him. 'His parents had money. I thought he was spoiled. When we graduated high school, he went to college and I had to get a job.' But, when Mike's parents bought him a brand new Chevy for a Christmas present his freshman year of college, Helen jokes she suddenly found Mike very interesting.

Mike wanted to show off his new car and Helen finally agreed to go on a date with him. 'I know our parents didn't like it, which made it even more exciting.' They went out a few times during his school break, and even wrote to each other while he was at college. Finally summer came, and Mike was back.

'It was really all about the car,' Helen shared. 'I felt like a million bucks driving around with Mike. My parents didn't have a car nearly as new or nice; no one I knew did. He was just a kid, and he had this incredible car. Mike was nice, but he really was just a spoiled kid. Still, we were having fun upsetting our parents and just driving around.'

Mike did get his share of speeding tickets, but Helen insists she made him slow down a bit when she was driving with him. 'I wanted to be seen, not in a drag race. So when I was in the car, he kept things under control.' Except the one night he didn't.

That night they were returning from a party in Brattleboro, Vermont. It was around midnight and Mike drove on Arch Street and, instead of slowing down, he drove faster. Helen screamed at Mike 'Mike too fast! Slow down now!' She says she was angry, not frightened.

Mike didn't slow down, he drove even faster. Helen became even angrier; she thought he was just showing off, trying to scare her. She says she hit him on the arm and he turned and smiled at her. It was then that she saw that he wasn't Mike anymore. The face that lit up from the dashboard lights was that of a skull. 'It was a grinning skull. It just looked at me. Then the car went even faster.'

Helen wasn't wearing a seatbelt. 'We just didn't do that. It isn't like things are today.' She looked up and saw the railroad tunnel ahead. She was desperate, so she opened her door, and rolled out into what she hoped was the soft side of the road. She broke her leg in several places, and is left with a slight limp today.

Mike hit the bridge. He lived, Helen assures me, but his hospital stay was much longer than hers. She said the passenger side of the car, what she calls the 'Suicide seat, that's what we called it, as more people die in that seat than any other in a car,' was crushed. 'I would have been dead if I hadn't jumped.'

Helen refuses to drive the road. 'I won't go through the tunnel. I'll drive around, but I won't go near that tunnel!'

There were other stories about skulls and apparitions associated with this stretch of road. Helen's was the most dramatic. Is it just an open area where it's easy to daydream and forget to watch your speed? Or are there other forces trying to control drivers who decide to take the scenic route?

Morning Mystery Moaner of Main Street

Keene's Main Street is famous for many things. It is claimed to be the widest Main Street in the United States, and people come from around the world to attend Pumpkin Fest where carved pumpkins line the street and town square.

Lesser known is an odd sight seen only very early in the morning. Folks out early on Main Street, before shops open and when the sun is just coming up, share Main Street with a mysterious spirit.

'I go for my walk early during the summer, before it gets too warm,' said one man. 'It was about 6 AM, and the street was quiet except for one other person. I was nervous as it seemed to be a homeless person, or someone mentally unsound. The person was dressed in rags, and shuffled along making moaning sounds.'

Downtown Keene is a good location for those who have physical difficulties. Someone who depends on a wheelchair or walker won't have difficulty accessing the many restaurants and stores. The sidewalks and crossing lights make downtown Keene, a very attractive area to live for those with limited mobility.

However, the morning mystery man has one very big difference than the average resident. Whenever anyone gets too close to him, he disappears.

Another resident said that the moaning shuffler made him nervous, therefore avoided him. One day he decided to stop judging and say 'hello.' When he crossed the street, to his surprise, the morning moaner disappeared. The jogger found the man across the street, the side he had just come from. He assumed the moaner had crossed the street, but could not understand how he could have done so, so quickly.

It finally became a game to this jogger. He was determined to meet the morning moaner face to face, yet he could never seem to get close. He did notice that the mystery man was dressed quite shabbily. The clothing seemed worn even beyond what any homeless person would wear. He also noticed that the mystery moaner was wearing no shoes. It was summertime, but on some cold mornings the jogger wondered how the man could stand the cold.

Finally the jogger became so frustrated, and frightened, that he changed his morning run route to avoid Main Street.

Most eyewitnesses don't think the morning moaner is a ghost. They think he is a homeless person, down on his luck, and wants to be left alone. There is much about the man that makes people want to avoid him; his eerie moaning, his shuffling steps, his hunched over shoulders and head might be enough to keep most people away, but there is also something more. Most folks said they felt slightly afraid of him, and it went beyond simple appearance. Some people wanted to go and offer even just a kind word to the obviously disturbed person, but something holds them back. Some describe getting goose bumps whenever they see this sad, unhappy spirit, and that fear overcomes their natural inclination to help.

The Main Street Moaner has only been seen on Keene's wide Main Street and has a talent for staying far away from others. A few report him as a shadowy, bent figure in a doorway, but no one has ever been able to get close enough to see what his features look like.

The figure is also only seen in spring, summer and fall. It's possible he is also out in winter, but that there are fewer residents out so early, or that in the cold, people hurry along too quickly to see a shadowy figure dressed in rags.

If the figure is not human, but a ghost, what could it be? When asked, an old-timer, and lifetime resident of Keene, gave a laugh and claimed the moaner was the disturbed brother of a local carpenter from long ago. The carpenter would bring his brother along with him on jobs, so that he could keep an eye on him. The brother wouldn't wash, was dressed poorly, and could only communicate by moaning. The senior remembers stories of this sad brother from his own father.

He wouldn't explain further, other than he had heard of this moaning, sad, spirit shuffling up and down Main Street his entire life. The Morning Mystery Moaner of Main Street is either very old indeed, or a ghost.

John

John Finds a Home, but Needs his Mother

There is a home on a quiet side-street just off of the Chesterfield road, about three miles west of Keene. It is a white, two-story home; a simple, box design built around 1840. There is an old barn nearby, slightly neglected, and a small, newer, two-car garage. There are large trees in the front yard and, in the summer, their full foliage blocks the sun and view of the front windows of the house.

But in winter, when the leaves are off the trees, you can see into the upstairs window. If you look at the window in the upper left corner of the house, you will see light-blue curtains. Sometimes you will also see a small boy. Just tall enough to look out, he can be seen peeking through the gap in the curtains. People would sometimes mention the boy to the homeowners, an older couple, asking if a grandchild was visiting. The couple would always claim the viewer must be mistaken; perhaps it was their large dog that had been looking out the window and the subject was always quickly changed.

This is the story of a little boy lost in a snowstorm.

The daughter of the couple who lived at the house decided to share this story. Though it does not take place in Keene, the town is involved as it is where this little boy so desperately wants to go. That is, if he is truly a ghost, and not just the imaginings of a lonely, elderly couple.

I'll call the daughter 'Amy', though that is not her name; her parents will be 'Sam and Jane'. According to Amy, her parents called her from their home one snowy, winter night, upset that their cat was missing. Amy is one of five children the couple raised in the home. She felt when all the children grew up and moved out, her parents transferred much of their concern and affection to their pets, a cat and black lab. Her parents wanted her to come over to help look for their missing cat and Amy refused, saying that it was too dangerous for her to drive in the storm. She advised them to stay home, as the cat would probably find someplace to hide.

Sam and Jane, after checking the garage and the barn, decided to take their truck and drive into the storm to look for the cat. They told Amy later what happened next, but only many years later when they were near death.

Jane was the first to see the little boy. He was standing near a bush by the side of the road. The bush was covered with snow, but oddly the little boy was not. He was wearing a dark suit, and wore an odd, dark hat on his head; not really proper attire for a blizzard. No gloves were on his hands, but he did have on high-top leather shoes.

Sam stopped the truck, concerned that such a young child would be out so late and in a storm. The little boy did not answer their questions about who he was or why he was out all alone, late at night, but he pointed to under the bush. When Sam looked to where the boy was pointing, he saw the family cat, shivering and hiding. Sam picked up the cat, and told the boy to get into the truck and warm up.

The little boy didn't seem cold, and he refused to talk. Sam and Jane rushed him back home, where they sat him down in their kitchen and covered him with a blanket. They tried to call the police to report the lost boy, but the phone was out of order. They had lost power, so they lit candles and made a fire. A small bed was made for the boy in front of the fire, and Amy's parents settled down near him for the night. They were concerned about how his family must have been feeling. After much begging from Jane, he finally spoke and told her his name was John Moore and said, 'I need to get to Keene. My mother and I are going to Keene. I think she is waiting for me there.'

The power was still out when the family awoke. John refused to eat or drink, and when they joked that he could not watch TV, he seemed confused. Jane was perplexed by his clothing, which he refused to remove. She also noticed he did not need to use the bathroom. She did brush his hair, and sat him on her lap and washed his face. Sam noticed he seemed clean, even though he had been through a very rough night. They speculated that John was from some Amish family, as he seemed to not understand about television. When Sam brought out the radio with batteries to listen to the news, the little boy seemed scared.

That morning Sam and Jane decided to drive to the police department to report finding the boy. Sam cleaned off the driveway, and warmed up the truck. Jane went to find an old coat from one of her children for John.

When she came back into the living room where he had been sitting, he was gone. Sam and Jane panicked. They searched the house and looked outside for footprints. There were none to be found. They didn't know what to do. Instead of driving to the police department, they decided to talk about what had happened. It was many years later when Amy's parents told her of that conversation.

They talked about how John seemed unlike other boys; how he wasn't cold despite the snow and wind; how he didn't eat or drink anything; how he wouldn't take off his clothing; and mostly how he just seemed so calm despite being away from his mother. Sam and Jane decided that he was not a normal little boy, but a ghost. Amy tried to get more details from her parents. How could they not tell the police about a little boy found in a snowstorm? All they could say was, 'You weren't there. We think we knew the entire time.'

Amy's parents didn't give up on John. 'For some reason, my parents felt this little boy needed them. I worried perhaps they had gone a little crazy, later in life. Perhaps they had invented this little boy as they missed having their children living with them.'

The next week, there was another snowstorm and Sam and Jane decided to look for John. They found him near where they found him before. This time Sam picked him up and tucked the boy in between himself and Jane. 'You are coming home with us,' he told John. He drove back to their house, and this time they had power. Still, John seemed to prefer a candle to electric lighting. They took John up to their youngest son's room, and put him in the bed, with a candle burning by his bedside. The next morning, Sam and Jane were glad to find John was still there.

Amy began to get suspicious when she would come over to visit, usually about once a week for dinner. Amy's siblings all lived out of state, and she was the only one still living in New Hampshire. Amy moved back to be near her mom and dad when she divorced. She'd gone upstairs once to find an old book she read as a child, and looked in her brother's old room. She was surprised to find a candle burning on a table by the bed. And the room, instead of being full of her brother's old stuff, was filled with simple toys and there was a soft, newly-made quilt on the bed. 'It was like stepping back in time,' Amy said.

'I felt I wasn't alone, as though I had interrupted someone. There was a teddy bear on the bed, and wooden blocks on the floor. There were puzzles on the bookshelf and all the books were old. There wasn't even a lamp in the room, just a candle.'

Amy talked to her parents, and they confessed about John Moore. They told of bringing him home after the second storm, and setting up a bedroom he would feel comfortable in. 'Sometimes he comes downstairs, and your father and I take turns reading to him,' Jane told Amy. Most of the time, John just stayed in his room. 'I can hear him playing, and he likes it if I stop in. We'll build with his blocks,' her father told her. John didn't like anything too modern or new. Electronic games perplexed him, and he would often stare out the window if a large truck or motorcycle went by. The family had learned that John would stay, as long as he wasn't too confused. If the family tried to introduce him to the modern world, he would leave. They would then have to wait for the next bad snowstorm to find him again.

'He needs us,' Jane told her daughter. 'We have to live quietly. He needs to have a home.' Amy was upset, and tried to get her parents to talk to their doctor about the situation, but they refused. 'I think more than the little boy needing them, they needed him.'

Their lives changed; Sam and Jane no longer went on vacations or trips together. Only one would visit their children at a time. Amy was the only family they had over; she was the only one they shared their secret with. They also became distant from their neighbors. They didn't like anyone asking about the little boy at the window; their life revolved around John and keeping his existence a secret.

Amy was sad, but also didn't want people to know that her parents thought they were living with a ghost. She did worry about why the little boy needed to go to Keene, if he did indeed exist. She played along, though. Amy convinced her parents to again try to get John to talk about his life. John said he and his mother were traveling to Keene on the train, when the accident happened. He could not find his mother. If only he could get to Keene he could find his mother and go back home. Amy worried, if by any chance John did exist, her parents were keeping John from finding his mother. She said that is when she hoped John wasn't real. The thought of a lost, little boy waiting for his mother broke her heart. She was never quite sure while her parents were alive.

One day Amy got a call from her mother. Her father had a stroke and was at the hospital. Amy hurried over, and Amy was upset as her mother had to go home to John. "I was so angry. Here was my father dying and my mom just worried about a ghost!" Even more bizarre, when Amy's father could finally speak, he kept saying he wanted to go home. He told Amy he wanted to die in John's room. 'Maybe I could guide him back home; if I am there when I die, I could take his hand and walk him to heaven with me.' Sadly, Sam was in no condition to go home and died quietly, a few days later. Amy was alone with her father, as her mother refused to come, but for only a few hours each day.

Amy grew angry with the ghost. Her mother became feebler after her husband's death. Jane became depressed that Sam had not been able to guide John to his mother. Amy had many fights with her mother, and threatened to have her evaluated. This is something she regrets, as her mother took an overdose of pills after one of their fights, and died in John's room. Amy thinks perhaps Jane wished to somehow guide John, and thought if she died in his room she could finish the job her husband wished to do.

While she never believed in John while her parents were alive, Amy believes in him now. She moved into her parent's house, and soon found she was not alone. She goes to John's room, and finds the toys rearranged. Things in the kitchen and living room move about. If she turns on the TV, it often just turns off. John seems to dislike her cell phone ringing, as she will find it hidden under cushions and once in the trash can.

The final proof for Amy was once, while raking leaves, she looked up at the window of John's room and saw him standing there. She knew her parents had been right all along. Amy believes that because her mother committed suicide, she was not permitted to guide John to heaven. And that they were also wrong to bring John back to live with them. Maybe Sam and Jane should have tried to drive him to Keene instead of having him live with them in order to ease their loneliness.

Amy is now investigating a train crash of over 150 years ago where, a little boy from Walpole traveling to Keene, died. She's going to find out which station the train was going to, and where that station is now. She hopes, if she can just take the little boy to wherever that train was going, his mother might be waiting. So now Amy also waits...she is waiting for the first big snowstorm, close in time to the train crash. She's going to drive her father's old truck and hopes to get John into the truck with her and drive him to Keene. Maybe, just maybe, his mother will still be waiting. Amy says it's time for John to go back home.

Downtown Ghostly Bowling Alley

There is a store on Main Street where soft music plays. The music is supposed to be left on at all times, even through the night, so that when an employee opens the store in the morning, she does not hear the sounds the music hides.

If you're a regular customer, you'll have an opportunity to hear the sounds the music masks. First, the employee turns down the music and, if you stand in just the right place, you hear the sounds. You will hear a muted rolling, followed by a sound of something being knocked over. And, if you listen carefully, you might even hear footsteps and the voices of men. It sounds very much like a modern bowling alley, only very muted and the balls and pins have the distinct sound of falling on a wooden floor. And it's not just the sound; the floor vibrates upon occasion. The sounds, the vibrations, could be from outside. Or perhaps the source comes from down below. Opening the door to the basement, you will smell the distinct odor of stale cigar smoke. The owner of the business will tell you it's just fumes from cars passing by or perhaps something to do with mold and damp.

It's believed there was, at one time, a bowling alley in the basement of the building. Bowling was a well-known, early pastime in Keene. These were simple alleys; pin boys set up the old wooden pins, which were much smaller than those used today. More of a gentlemen's get together, bowling was a popular form of recreation. Possibly even today, bowling is popular with some resident ghosts who still show up at their favorite bowling alley to enjoy an eternal game or two.

The music plays still plays softly, just loud enough to cover the slight sound of the game, though nothing can cover up the gentle rumble that comes up whenever a strike is bowled.

The Eternal Tenant

Stories of life after death are often ambiguous, based upon eyewitness testimony and perhaps a fuzzy photograph or strange video. The story that most impressed the staff at the Cheshire County Historical Society was that of one ghost, reported by two different people.

A tenant of an apartment in an old house came into the Historical Society to research the history of his apartment. He'd seen an apparition of a woman; she wore an old-fashioned dress and sat by the window, looking out at the street. The tenant wasn't afraid of the woman, but he wanted to know more about her. The Historical Society was glad to look up the history of the building, although there is no official record of ghosts or hauntings. The tenant went home and was not heard from again.

Many years later, another man came to the Historical Society to research his home. He had seen a 'ghostly woman' wearing an old-fashioned dress. She, too, was sitting at a window, looking out at the street. This story sounded familiar to the staff and, upon checking the address, it was indeed the same apartment. This tenant also had no fear of the ghost. He simply wished to know about the eternal tenant in his apartment.

The people of Keene are very tolerant and accepting of sharing their homes with previous occupants. No other tenants from this apartment have shown up. It could be that the last tenant to check with the Society is still living there, perfectly happy to pay rent for both himself and the ghost. The mysterious spirit, like most Keene ghosts, is welcome to stay as long as she likes.

Nighttime Specter

Beaver Mill's Specter

A retirement home on Railroad Street is the location of probably the most horrifying ghost reported in Keene. This story comes from a young woman we'll call Beth. Beth heard this story from her late grandmother 'Mary', who lived in the retirement home. Mary often had trouble sleeping at night and walking helped her to relax. She would take advantage of the quiet of the late night and walk the halls of the building with her walker.

One day, when she was a child, Beth and her mother visited her grandmother. To their dismay they saw Mary's walker lying on its side in the hallway. The young woman remembers the panic in her mother's voice, as she banged on Mary's door and cried out, 'Mom! Are you alright?'

Her grandmother opened the door, shaking with fright. Beth's mom calmed Mary down and asked her why the walker was in the hall. Beth was spooked by the story her grandmother told.

Mary was doing her usual insomnia cure, a few steps up and down the hallway, when she noticed white smoke coming from the other end. Thinking there was a fire, she started back to her room to call for help, when she realized that it wasn't real smoke; it was more of a mist. Then, the building shook. Trembling, Mary stopped and peered at the mist, fearful of what would come next and what it would mean for herself and her fellow residents. Mary didn't have to wait long to find out.

Coming down the hallway, floating slightly above the mist, was a man. He glowed from within, and he appeared to be burned and bleeding. He reached his hand out to Mary. His good hand: well, the only hand. The other arm was almost completely gone. The man gave a low moan. Then, the stench of smoke reached Mary's senses. She quickly dropped her walker and stumbled back into her room. Mary sat in her room the rest of the night, with her back to the door, shaking in fear.

Beth asked Mary why she didn't call the fire department. Her grandmother just shook her head and said, 'He wasn't real. He couldn't have been real.' It was then the young woman's mother realized she was there and sent her to another room. Mary never spoke of the incident again.

Our investigation turns up this interesting bit of history. The retirement home was built using material from the old Beaver Mill building. The Beaver Mill site would be a good candidate for a haunting or two. There was a horrible boiler explosion at the Beaver Mill building on May 22, 1893. Bricks from this explosion were found streets away. The explosion killed two instantly and one man was burned. It was truly a disaster; not only for the men killed, but those who had worked at the factory lost their jobs.

Some say ghosts are the apparitions of a tragic event, forever imprinted on a location because of the great grief associated with the site. If any site in Keene would have such ghosts, the retirement home built of the Beaver Mill would.

Where There's Smoke, There's Tom and Jack

Not all the ghosts of Keene are human. People often talk of a beloved pet, usually a cat or dog, they believe are still loyal companions long after the pet has died. Sounds of soft footpads, almost silent meows, and doors that open mysteriously are signs of a pet spirit. There are reports of a dog's barking, awakening its family to danger: only this is the eternal vigilance of a dog long dead, still protecting it's loved ones.

Tom and Jack weren't pets, but they did belong to the entire city of Keene. They were a beautiful set of gray horses, used to pull a fire engine. They helped save many lives and properties with their well-trained strength. The fire horse had to be a very special horse: strong to pull the engine, swift of speed was of the essence with a fire, and also brave, as most horses will shy and run away from fire and smoke. Tom and Jack were the pride of the Keene Fire Department for both their beauty and sense of duty. Photographs of the horses proudly marching in parades can be found in historic records.

Fire was especially frightening before the advent of smoke alarms and fire sprinkler systems. It was only under the watchful eye of a neighbor or sheer luck, if a fire was discovered at night. The amount of work to put out a fire often meant every citizen had to pitch in when needed. Residents of Keene were required to own a certain number of leather buckets to be used in case of fire. Putting out fires was a concern for all, not just for the professional firefighter.

At one time, Keene was full of horses, conveniently located for their owners when needed. A tour of Keene today, shows how important the horse was to daily life before the advent of cars. There are many barns inside the city. Some are attached to homes and now serve as garages. Some Keene barns have been converted into apartments or homes.

Horses naturally avoid fire, and it was often the loud whinnies of panicked horses that warned folks that a fire had started. This is perhaps why, when horses were still fairly common in Keene, no one mentions the ghosts of Jack and Tom. Jack and Tom served Keene as some of the last fire horses, as 'horse-power' came to mean a motor and not an animal. 1920 was the last year fire horses were officially used in Keene.

Today, Jack and Tom may still be protecting the citizens of Keene. People report being alerted to fire by first, being awakened by the sound of a panicked horse, then the smell of smoke, and finally the awareness of a fire. Keene doesn't have many horses close to downtown, but reports of the sounds of horses awakening folks to a fire, persist.

One fire survivor reports what happened to him, 'I awoke to this loud screeching sound. I had no clue what it was, but could tell my house was filling with smoke. I got up quickly and awoke my family and we ran out of the house. We then looked up and I saw, in the smoke, the shape of two horses. Gray horses, gray like the smoke and fire. It was just the heads and front legs and then the shapes slowly disappeared as the flames grew.' The family survived, despite their smoke alarms not working, but the home was a complete loss.

It seems Jack and Tom cannot resist a fire of any type. People report seeing the shapes of two horses in smoke from other fires; sometimes even in a simple backyard bonfire or leaf burning. The description is always of seeing the shape of horses in the smoke, before the images quickly dissipate.

If you awake in the night to the sound of horses, pay attention and don't roll back to sleep. Tom and Jack might be trying to tell you something. Also, please make sure your smoke detectors are working, because to depend on ghostly intervention for fire protection is foolish indeed.

Anna Banks

Beware of Anna Banks: Cat, Dog or Demon

There is a lovely house near Gilsum Street, with a small, printed sign in the window near the front door that says 'BEWARE OF DOG'. The sign is faded from the sun and, if you ring the doorbell, you will not be greeted by a barking dog.

The house is home to yet another Keene animal ghost, but just what kind of animal this ghost is, depends on who you are. If you are a friend, you will meet Anna, a lovely jet-black cat of undetermined age. If you are a foe...beware!

A lovely family lives in the small, white house: mother, father, and two young children. They are the second-generation owners and the mother, Nora, grew up in the house. 'There was always a black cat when I was growing up. When my parents bought the house, they were told that a cat came with it. So, when my parents moved in, Anna the cat was already here.' She isn't sure if it's the same cat, but ever since Nora was born there has been a black cat at the house. When one of the Anna's gets old and dies, soon enough, another black cat shows up. 'This has only happened twice since I've lived here, but my mother said it happened once, before I was born.'

Nora said she asked her mother for more details about the black cats associated with the house. Her mother claimed that when they bought the house, the cat was part of the package. Nora's parents liked cats, though they probably would not have picked a black cat. The cat was a bit standoffish but good pet; then one day she grew thin and died. 'Mom thought the reason the cat came with the house was that Anna was pretty old already. The previous family probably thought the cat would be happier not moving.' Nora's mom buried the cat in the backyard. The family didn't need to wait long before the next Anna came along. This one, not more than a kitten, was sitting in the backyard near the old cat's grave a few mornings later.

At first, it was thought that the cat was dumped by someone who had heard the family had lost their cat. 'Plus,' Nora said, 'not everyone wants a black cat. Mom figured someone knew she'd accept another one.' This cat was also named Anna for no reason anyone can remember. Oddly enough, each death of an Anna has brought a new Anna to the home, usually within a week.

Nora tried to trace the history of the cats, she wondered if it extended even further into the history of the house. She found old photographs of the home, and sure enough, in many of the photographs dating back to the 1890's, there is a black cat. One elderly neighbor remembers a black cat named Anna at the home in the 1940's.

'Anna', laughed Nora a bit nervously, 'is very shy. She's always a she, and she likes only certain people.' While I was visiting, I was delighted when the current Anna came over and allowed me to pet her. Nora smiled and asked, 'Do you own a black cat?' I told her I now own a calico stray, found on the streets of Keene, but at one time I had owned a black cat named Othello. Nora just nodded her head, 'She really likes people who own or have owned black cats. We joke she's a demon cat, but we can't help but like having her around.' Nora then shared other peculiar things about the cats. 'For one thing, if the cat goes in the yard, all the other animals leave. You won't find birds or squirrels around. Even dogs and other cats leave her alone. Anna has never been in a fight and seems to like to be alone. We just never have had another pet. Anna seems to be happiest alone and I'm busy enough with two children.'

Who needs a dog when you have Anna? Nora points out that this is what she's heard from others, but people claim that her family must own a black dog. 'I've gone away, and some of the neighbors say they heard our dog barking in the middle of the night. I know we don't have a dog, but they swear they've heard ferocious barking and even come out to see if everything is alright. Once, a couple of teenagers were seen running away from the house. We think maybe they were going to break in, but they heard this dog barking and left.'

Anna just looked at me for more petting, as if proud of her barking abilities. 'We even get those door-to-door religious people.' Nora pauses then decides to share the rest, 'If I'm upstairs busy, I sometimes hear barking, and I'll look out and it's those Bible people, you know who I mean.' They quickly leave when they hear the 'demon dog.' Nora assures me, to her it's only a quiet barking and growl. Nora says that the door-to-door salesmen of anything from candy bars to religion must hear something much more frightening than she does, judging by their quick exit from her front door. Nora says even if Anna is a demon and not a ghost, she seems to have the best interests of the house in mind. Nora also joked since her daughter is a Girl Scout, Anna never growls at those who stop by selling cookies.

Nora started putting up the Beware of Dog sign years ago if they were going out of town. 'I want to give anyone wanting to break in here fair warning. There aren't any 'Beware of Demon Cat' signs that I can find. I can find joke 'Beware of Cat' signs, but I need one that really means stay away.' Anna seemed just fine with my visit, especially as I brought her one of my hand-knit catnip mice.

Anna, the black demon cat, seems happy to stay near Gilsum Street. 'Black cats may be scary to others, but we enjoy taking care of her.' Nora said. Her mother had heard rumors that the first Anna was saved on All Hallows Eve from children intent on tormenting it, by a fortune teller who used to live in the area named Anna Banks.

Nora isn't so sure, 'that would have had to be a long time ago. Long before this house was built.' But perhaps the spirit of one of Keene's most famous fortune tellers, Anna Banks, still resides in the shape of a never-ending series of black cats. If so, Nora and her family say any new Anna cats will always have a welcome home with them.

Monkey Ghost House

A home on a small street near downtown, is the residence of a simian ghost we'll name 'George'. The ghost of George inhabits a lovely home with a beautiful front porch and signs of his time there still exist. A playhouse stands in the backyard; the small, one-car garage, stores his old toys. In the basement, stands a large cage, which is peculiar enough to generate scary thoughts of what it might have contained.

George makes himself known in typical monkey fashion. He's known to tug at hair, especially long hair, as a person walks down the stairs or sits in the living room. The mischievous monkey will also throw poo at visitors he disapproves of...or perhaps for fun. Smells that are definitely scatagorical in nature are still reported.

No one seems to know why George might have decided to stay in Keene. It appears the monkey had a loving home with toys, outdoor play area and large indoor cage. Perhaps the monkey just had it too good, and isn't ready to leave such a pleasant home. Are the stories simply the fantasies of folks based on the stories of a former monkey resident? Or does George still reside and get up to trouble in Keene? The ghost monkey of Keene is probably one of the more colorful ghosts in the town. Just watch out if you have long hair. And if you smell anything foul? Duck!

Kitty Mervine is a New Hampshire artist and author. She's also known for accidentally creating one of the best ghost photographs taken in New Hampshire (with assistance from Travis Roy). She lives in Keene with her cat Moxie, who has been known to see ghosts, but, for the most part, just enjoys watching squirrels.

Noah Whippie is a New Hampshire artist known for his detailed and intricate illustrations. His illustrations can be found almost everywhere, including books, decks of cards and his own comic book series.

Made in the USA
Las Vegas, NV
24 March 2022

46224665R00040